The Fabulous Beasts

THE
Fabulous
Beasts

Poems by JOYCE CAROL OATES

Illustrations by A. G. Smith, Jr.

LOUISIANA STATE UNIVERSITY PRESS

Baton Rouge and London

The poems published here have appeared previously in the following periodicals, sometimes in slightly different forms: *Beloit Poetry Journal, Brushfire, Canadian Forum, Esquire, Fiction Midwest, Hudson Review, Little Magazine, Mademoiselle, Malahat Review, Modern Poetry Studies, Ohio Review, Poem, Poetry Northwest, Prairie Schooner, Prism International, Quarry* (Ontario, Canada), *Quarry* (Santa Cruz), *Queen's Quarterly, Seneca Review, Southern Review, Southwest Review, Sparrow, Strivers Row, Today's Poets.*

A broadside of "In Case of Accidental Death" was published in a limited edition by the Pomegranate Press, and a group of poems under the title *Dreaming America* was published in a limited edition by Aloe Editions. "Wooded Forms" appeared as a limited edition published by the Albondocani Press.

To all these acknowledgment and thanks are due.

"Seizure" was included in the *Borestone Mountain Poetry Awards for 1973*.

ISBN 13: 978-0-8071-0285-5

Library of Congress Catalog Card Number 74–27198
Copyright © 1975 by Joyce Carol Oates
Illustrations copyright © 1975 by A. G. Smith, Jr.

1977 printing

This book was designed by Dwight Agner. It was set in Sabon, a type face designed by Jan Tschichold, by Graphic Composition, Inc., Athens, Georgia. The book was printed by Thomson-Shore, Inc., Dexter, Michigan.

for my friend Elizabeth Graham

A tenth of an inch's difference,
And heaven and earth are set apart.
　　　　　　—the Heart Sutra

Contents

III   *The Child-Martyr*

IV *The Fabulous Beasts*

I *Broken Connections*

Broken Connections

Are you safe there? Can you hear me?
Across the snow-maddened miles
we shout questions and answers.
The air is choppy as a river.
He is saying, *Can you hear—*
as the telephone line crackles, like laughter,
then goes dead.
It is dead.

Nothing to do but replace the receiver,
like this.
If the line is dead it is totally dead.
There is no deadness like it.

Nothing to do but put on a jacket,
go out onto the porch to watch the storm.
Pockets of snowy air explode from pine boughs,
the porch's screen bells inward,
snow-stubbled grass runs to bloom somewhere
out of sight. . . .
There are animal-shapes in shadows,
in silence.
Though the land here is deeded
it is unknown: it is silent.

It is not your storm,
it is not your life.
Not a way of explaining the churning sky,
your quiet panic,
your curious smile of betrayal.
Your life is not prose:
you didn't write it.
You don't even have to understand it.

The wind blows all night
now that the telephone cable failed
and words cannot be used.
You are here.
Your soul softens gradually, recognizing
the air, the snow, the silence
of broken connections.

After Terror. . . .

      . . . we move like the slow
reverent fingers of the blind.
Our maneuvering of what remains of us is a prayer
worked out in flesh.
We pray to what has not yet happened.

Cautious, we decipher the code that surrounds us.
It is all protein, all oxygen, all new.
It is interior as the roofs of our mouths.

The Impasse

In the ditches, in the dark crevices,
shrunken glaciers keep their chill.
You cannot step across.
The cold radiates upward, even against the sun,
and you cannot step across—
a few feet, a few inches—
you fear the tremor of ice
and what is not human.

Over there—an ordinary furrowed field.

You cannot step across
yet you cannot go back.
You cannot move at all.
The long meandering fingers of ice will thicken,
winter upon winter.

Later you may say *How cowardly I was!*
Now you think *Even this is my strength.*

Wonders of the Invisible World

A northwest wind has maddened the river.
Waves churn and flatten and lose themselves in ripples —
Swirling in frantic half circles—
Breaking on the high-banked ice—

Yesterday the river ran swiftly to the east.
Now it plunges everywhere, drowning.

A small brown-painted box rocks in the wind.
It turns from side to side in that nameless tree—turns halfway,
    turns back.
Empty, its roofs sloped like the roofs of our house.
Where are the birds? Hidden everywhere.

> There are absences heavy as the ceilings in old houses,
>   thick-beamed, built too low.
> There are memories thinly poisonous as the smoke of old
>   wood-burning stoves.
> There are slashes in the flesh that become eccentric scars.

That noise in the brush alongside the house?
Sparrows, invisible.

> A woman is forbidden abstraction.
> She must heal; she must touch.
> She must braid us all together.
> By love, as by roots in the soil, we will be connected to
>   one another.
> We will not fly off the surface of the earth and drown in the
>   Void: so secretly rooted.
> But the connections must be underground,
> Such wonders performed invisibly.

> If you are not wonder-working,
> Who will have you?

A Posthumous Sketch

—for Colin Wilson

The challenge: to conquer the element that had drowned my friend.

From Aurora Borealis reeling spiraling to earth, unmelted Ice Age shapes swept upon us in this cove, usually sheltered from the wilder sea, and it was as if immense hulks of Beings were sleepwalking through that day and nearly all of that night—"most severe storm damage in forty-three years"—and of course my friend S. drowned. A week later, he had not been found. Parts of the boat were salvaged along eleven miles of coastline; several other boats went down, but no human being drowned that afternoon except S. Strangely enough, after the gale winds subsided, all was serene and blue-tinted and the sun and clouds appeared in a harmonious relationship, yes, like malleable clogs of edible substance in a sky-blue bowl, a cereal bowl, which one might fancifully push into ever-new patterns with a spoon, smiling all the while. If I had surrendered to a soul-shattered weeping for S., the clearing of the storm would have exposed me aged and untimely.

Ten days passed. The telephone rang one morning and, resigned, I answered it. I knew. It could be no surprise. I hardly listened to the voice that spoke to me, informing me of "a body" that had been located, except to take directions: my mind is keen, razor-keen, and often operates without my noticing. The voice bade me farewell gravely, and there was a click at the other end of the line. Saddened but owning in myself a proper instinct for my own animal-magnetic cunning, I did not hang up at once. There was no dial tone. Yet there was no silence—a muffled babbling of many voices, women's voices, telephone operators up and down the coast, clickings, breathings, odd mechanical disturbances; yet still I waited, in patience though I had been wakened from sleep and stood now half-naked in my drafty kitchen; and finally I heard or seemed to hear my friend S.'s voice, words which brightened the shade-drawn dimness about me: *Let us together solve the great mystery!*

I hung up, abruptly. I shuddered.

I took the highway and not the beach road; the beach road winds and twists, it is shocking, lovely, ill paved, very jolting to the spirit and meant only for healthy bodies. I drove quickly, twenty miles above the speed limit, on the practical wide dry highway.

I had no trouble locating them. They were standing self-consciously on the beach, awaiting my arrival. It was a clear, chilly day though the official month was now July; but no matter the official month, you cannot set yourself against the ocean currents, or against the squalls and demonic thunderstorms that swing down from the Arctic, though you may well laugh and shut your eyes in the manner of my friend S.

He had tested the element many times, to the very point of breaking, and the soiled, frayed sail had at last shuddered into the lengthening waves. His seventeen-foot sailboat was old, but the sea was older. S. had always joked about the boat, claiming to be ashamed of it; he was very poor and the boat was, I believe, a gift made to him by some stranger; yet obviously he loved his boat, enough to go out sailing every afternoon though he could not swim and declared that he abhorred the water.

A delicate untidy youth, he had always lain in bed late in the morning; in recent years he slept later and later, and confided in me that he so dreaded his afternoon sail (never embarked upon later than two-thirty) that he tried to sleep as late as possible, so as to shorten the hours of wakeful apprehension. I responded at once by roaring: *A macabre mad sense of humor!* In this fashion I attempted to deny him the wit of his own predicament, which inspired at times an irrational envy in me (for he gloated he should die before me and force me to age simply by his premature example) and though I loved him I half loathed him, as you may understand. And so I would roar with laughter at his melancholy sentiments, and shrivel my handsome countenance with thought when he jested, which was often enough, for he was a slender untidy wealthy-minded young man. Laughter is a holy language, which we do not bestow too freely; I hoarded my holiness. S. stated that he could hoard nothing, but yearned to mate his spirit with all of the world—and an almost physical distress would come upon him, a lust of the spirit, so that his eyes would fill with tears. At such times I would offer him a cigar.

Uniformed men awaited me. No, four were in uniform—State Police—and two were not, two were merely natives from the area. The scene had already arranged itself before my arrival, and showed a deficiency of imagination. A boy of about fourteen, a hulking child-faced boy, stood nervously off to one side, in clothes too large for him; probably the person who had "discovered the body." A soiled strip of canvas lay on the beach, evidently covering something; evidently covering the body. The canvas looked like part of a sail, and was very dirty.

And I? A surprising sight for 8:15 A.M. of a somewhat overcast Tuesday morning two miles north of the townlet of Loon Isle (such are the names up here!), in freshly laundered white shorts and a magenta pullover shirt, its collar open, a varicolored pastel scarf about my throat, not so vivid in its shades as to throw into sickly contrast my pale complexion. I wore excellent sandals, of a carefully tooled leather, each thong thick and firm. I had brushed my hair hard, in honor of death, and though my hand had so trembled as to make shaving difficult, I had shaved my face in a normal fashion, and had smoothed it with a mint-perfumed lotion. My eyes revealed no dread or revulsion, but only my usual civilized stare.

And so I was prepared to "identify the body."

Yet when one of the State Troopers drew the canvas away, a terrible event took place: I laughed. I heard myself laugh. And I heard these utterly uncharacteristic, amazing words come forth from my own throat: "Is that a human body? *That?* Oh, why, you've waked me up for nothing—this is a sheep's carcass—or a dog's— *That* a human body, what a joke!" I stepped forward to investigate more closely. It seemed to me that no one was in charge here; rudderless and sail-drooping the moment lay about us, and no one but I might seize control. So I peered at the carcass with more care. "Let me see the jaw of it. Where is the face? Why is the face gone? I can recognize anyone I have known by his teeth . . . I always watch the lips and the mouth . . . gentlemen, you understand how the lips and the mouth reveal truths to us which the tongue and the eyes try to conceal. . . . "

A great dizziness rose up to me. The carcass had no face, and yet it seemed to possess a certain facial expression. It peered up at me. A sheep! A dog! A stranger! While the men stared at me in total astonishment I drew together by sheer strength all the outward-soaring filaments of my soul, I refused to lose consciousness and sink beside *that*, on so ugly a beach, I sucked in my breath so that my stomach contracted inside the magenta shirt . . . now that I have passed my thirtieth birthday, my stomach has grown flabby, my entire body is aging and sinking me into the fifth or sixth decade of my life . . . yet to be so old, so quickly! How has it happened?

Around me were the scandalized thought-waves of these good citizens.

And so I recovered. I said, "Yes, it's him . . . yes. . . . I don't know what came over me. Gentlemen, it is my friend; I admit it. I recognize him . . . I admit it . . . I know the jacket, yes, it's him . . . no mistake. . . ."

The moment was therefore somewhat redeemed. I wanted to be able to weep, because in their cold hating hearts these men did not expect it of me. They stared in hatred at a stranger in white shorts and a magenta shirt, with hairy legs, not one of them, not a native of this place; if not my clothes and my bearing, my manner of speaking would surely identify me as a stranger. It is well known that summer residents of this area are despised, though their money is welcomed eagerly enough! I noticed a clean-shaven young police officer flash a truly savage contemptuous look at me, as if about to utter: *Serves your friend right; you're next!*

The boy edged away from us adults, frightened and ashamed. S. would have regretted disturbing the child with his corpse, so ruinful of an ordinary Tuesday morning. I stared and stared and yet could not weep. *Weep, you must weep! The occasion demands tears!* And yet I could not force myself to weep, some terror had risen in me, some icy impotence out of the North. . . .

Fish-nibbled, mocking in his lost beauty, handless and faceless my friend S. . . . *My God, why did I answer that telephone?*

And then, clarity.

The newspapers provide clarity in our time. As soon as I glanced at the Avedon *Observer,* a slightly smudged but reliable weekly paper published in a town fifteen miles to the south, in that very instant I felt my trembling cease, for any tragedy that can be explained in ten inches of type cannot be a profound one. I unfolded the *Observer* and read quickly of S.'s death, the broken boat, the salvaged wreckage, yes, yes, and photographs of several fishermen with items discovered along the rocky edge of the sea—perhaps the various parts would add up to a boat, like a jigsaw puzzle in three dimensions?—but it is highly doubtful that the natives would surrender their puzzle parts, for such items would rightly be cherished as souvenirs.

S.'s photograph was a poor one. I myself had provided it, and it was the only snapshot of him I had—he was shy of cameras, and indeed this photograph quite distorted his slender face, causing the eyes to appear even larger than they were in real life; he looked barely sixteen (he had been twenty-five at the time the picture was taken), and his shapely lips were gone in an overexposed blur, and gone too his timid-suspicious smile.

I folded the newspaper up carefully and laid it aside.

This event occurred at the meal called breakfast. Since my appetite cannot function before early afternoon, I eat my meal of breakfast between the hours of one and two, usually; a proper time of day to sip a very light, tart wine, though if the day is actually hot I will have a pint or two of beer. But I must say that this summer has been disappointingly somber. I folded the *Observer*, laid it aside, sighed wearily. . . . By the position of the sun I was forced to calculate that it must now be nearly three o'clock. I had risen at noon and spent some time in the bathtub, for the inward trembling had seemed to call for therapeutic applications, but now that the trembling had largely ceased I felt unaccountably weary. How long this summer was!

Then, for some reason, I stood and left the cottage and strolled down to the beach.

I did not know why, I did not know what beckoned to me. But almost immediately I felt a strange certainty . . . something would happen, perhaps something would reveal itself to me . . . in me there has always been, from earliest youth, a caginess entirely of the body, which often operates quite independently of my mind . . . and though I had gained weight over the years, particularly around my midriff, I still possessed the gait of a man with a graceful soul.

The waves broke on the shore. Wave after wave. Lengthening as I stared, and then contracting, squeezing together, breaking . . . and then lengthening again. . . . One night I had wandered along this stretch of beach, and the waves had whispered: *Acedia. Acedia. Acedia.* Not to be tormented by such an ode I lit a cigar and refused to retreat to the safety of my bed, and finally brazened out the whispering, a small triumph but not a negligible one. But this afternoon the waves did not whisper. They were very noisy, robust. From the choppy seesawing horizon they flowed to me and broke at my feet, and I mouthed to myself words that imparted a bittersweet taste to my tongue:

> . . . As when heaved anew
> Old ocean rolls a lengthened wave to the shore,
> Down whose green back the short-lived foam, all hoar,
> Bursts gradual with a wayward . . . a wayward . . . a wayward. . . .

I paused, unable to complete the line. *A wayward. . . .*

Wayward?

I stared out into the water and something compelled me, suddenly, to step into it. Cold, very cold! Very inhospitable! Yet if I wanted to complete that line I must seek out S., who had uttered it; I must, to surpass him, test the strength of this element that had drowned him. A wayward delight. A wayward *triumph.* Yes, as the young police officer had almost said aloud, *You're next!*

In a sudden vertiginous strength I filled my lungs with the cold damp manly air of the sea: in the face of all dangers, all mysteries, I become uncommonly clear to myself, as if the transparencies of my melancholy and my cheer mated to form some stern unbreakable substance. *There is that within me which shall tire Torture and Time, and breathe when I expire.* . . . Ah yes! Yes! And so, after glancing up and down the beach to affirm my solitude, and noting that no human figure disturbed this windy scene, and that the only evidence of humanity apart from my own rented cottage was a long-abandoned lighthouse a half-mile away, I began with solemnity the stripping of my body: a sacred ritual, which must be performed with an utter chastity of precision. My body shivered, but whether with the cold or with healthy excitement I did not know.

Slowly undressing I stared at the waves and summoned up a vision of my friend S., that soggy little denim jacket of his I had always despised, and begged him to cast away; the fish-nibbled face and hands; the angelic glimmer of his face, so dazed by the darker angels that had hovered about him in life (ah, if there were time to speak of the random deaths of women,whom S. loved yet could not give birth to!); the glistening rapidity of his walk, which at times startled me, for he seemed to approach me from a corner of my own eye, totally

14

unimagined by anything in me. . . . I had annoyed him with a nickname, "The Snake," for when he strode barefoot he reminded me of nothing so much as a serpent somehow walking on the tip of its tail—strange, rapid, remote his slightest movement—glistening, ubiquitous, and impossible to capture—even for me impossible to capture in the Protean turns of my language.

I would demonstrate to S. that I surpassed him; that immersing oneself in this element and returning were far more heroic than going down.

And now I stood naked, totally alone. All of mutable mankind was drawn up into me; yet I was alone. I had not swum for several weeks and, prior to that, I had not swum for more than a year, yet my body shivered with excitement as I stepped into the freezing surf. I marveled at the feel of the water, which was like another aspect of my own manhood, smooth and yet strong, like skin backed by hard muscle. Not a friendly element, the surf, and yet one which promised joy.

It was difficult to maintain my balance, so long as I waded out; then I began to swim, thrusting myself into the fiery-cold wave as it swept to me, and immediately I felt a response to my own solemnity. There was a kinship here. I began to swim: one stroke and then another . . . my left arm rising, my hand cutting the water sharply, and then cupping it . . . my right arm drawn lightly down against my side, and then rising . . . all in a rhythm I did not have to calculate, but needed only to recall. . . . And I recalled how, as a child, I had loved the water because it sheltered my lameness, and I had despised the level pavement of our cities because it singled me out, and for a defect no language could transfigure. It was no cause for wonder, then, that the water parted to accept me, to test me, and that I felt or seemed to feel small warm currents somehow inside the large freezing impact of the waves. My muscles strained, and began to ache; my breath was uneven; and yet I was not frightened.

Swimming out from land, swimming to sea: how one's manhood is honored! I seemed to be swimming into a great howling void that hid my deepest, truest self, as if descending into my own past.

Soon I saw that I was swimming alongside a boy, myself at the age of eleven years; he plowed ahead through the waves, ambitious but soon to tire. I, so many decades his elder, swam more cautiously, with full respect for the sanctity and danger of the sea. Cautiously, cautiously. One stroke and then the next . . . and then the next . . . I knew how to breathe and how not to breathe, and resisted gasping for air through my mouth. . . . Ah, the stagnation of my life fell from me and I wondered that I had not ventured into this astonishing void each day of my adulthood! My own oceanic self beckoned to me.

I knew then that there can be no accidents.

No accidents.

None in the ocean, and perhaps none on land. There are no accidents.

No accidents, no accidental drownings. S. dropped like a weight; he had yearned to do so, and had declared that he would make no vulgar attempt to combat the waves—not S. in his pride!—I, however, swam for more than a mile, and my eleven-year-old self dropped back, grew weary in an instant, began to choke, to drown; he disappeared from view and I forgot him. My body felt heavy. I was a weight propelled only by the exertion of my will. When I lifted my right arm high over my head I felt the first stab of pain in my side. . . . But I did not falter, I had to try the strength of this mad element that had drowned my friend. I had to triumph over it and over him. There came upon me a sense of power, a memory of an old melancholy thought I had once had of myself and my destiny: that it was my fatality to live, to wear inside myself (as if the body were hollow, and must be clothed) a strange barrenness of spirit. And so there could be no accidents, not in the universe I inhabited.

I grew faint. I began to see S. beneath me, a pale rival swimming effortlessly beneath the surface of the sea, sea serpent mocking me, a streaming paleness . . . smiling at me . . . transforming himself into a corpse iridescent with rot. . . . *Let us together solve the great mystery!* he cried. I shuddered with terror, yet hardened my heart. I swam over him.

I triumphed.

Returning to the shore was dangerous, a danger I had somehow not anticipated. One imagines that drowning is possible only when he is swimming out; yet the risk of drowning is perhaps greater when he is returning wearily to land, his body exhausted, his will slackening. There is the danger of relief, premature relief—a miscalculation of distance—an underestimation of the savage strength of the waves nearest the shore. But in my youth I had been an excellent swimmer and my old skill and caginess did not abandon me. Once again I swam over the glimmering withered body of my friend, whose torn lips seemed to shape a greeting to me, and whose hair foamed darkly, but I ignored the horror and swam with my eyes shut, my face tense to deny the exhaustion of my body and my soul.

You have no right to triumph over me! he cried.

And so I swam back to shore, staggering, vomiting; I began to vomit suddenly, and could not control the agony of my retching, and only the fact that I was able now to touch bottom saved me. I staggered. I fell to my hands and knees, and stumbled upright again. Water streamed down my naked body wildly; I had begun the trial in July and now, staggering back to shore, I believed that months, years, decades had passed. How exhausted I was! I stood alone on the beach, panting, shivering convulsively. I wiped at my eyes. The beach was wide and empty, my clothes were nowhere to be seen, the cottage I had rented looked somehow different, though I was too confused to ascertain what had been done to it. So many years had passed. . . . I made note of the lighthouse, which was still standing: a dull wind-worn tower on a small peninsula. I had begun my swim in the afternoon and now it was dusk. And to my amazement I saw a lamp burning up in the lighthouse, not a beam directed out to sea, but an ordinary domestic lamp. . . . Perhaps someone had bought the lighthouse to live in, perhaps he had been observing my struggle in the waves?

If that were so, what must he now be thinking? He must admire me!

For a long moment I stood in my triumph, my body heaving with the effort to take in air, my eyes fixed with a proud certainty upon that tower. Perhaps, even, a man and his wife had bought it, and both had observed my triumph over S. and over nature itself. . . . And now they would be marveling at my courage, they would perhaps take heart from my exertions and come to see what a noble enigma is man. . . .

Yet the tower gave no awareness of me; the small prim domestic lamp was no beam, anxious to illuminate my triumph; and I felt the moment pass mockingly, as all moments of my life had passed, pleasure swelling into satiety. There was an evil barrier between all I had experienced and my own soul, always, at the very height of my joy a premonition of the abyss—the greater the elevation I had attained, the more sudden and hopeless my fall—

I looked back to sea. And now the horror of my situation struck me: my friend S. was still there, still waiting. He was still there. Fish-pale, gleaming, glimmering like a serpent; more youthful than I, more evil. He awaited me in that unconquered element . . . *he* had triumphed, not I. And the ocean remained, unconquered. It gave no sign of me to myself. I might never have entered it, might never have been born, for all its rough noisy Being acknowledged of me.

I had conquered both S. and the ocean so long as I was swimming; but, as soon as I stepped out onto land, my magic died. I had not triumphed. I was a mortal man.

And so . . . and so I realized that there was nothing for me to do but return to the task: once more I must swim out, a good mile or more, over the body of my friend; once more I must take on that struggle, that endless struggle. I felt almost sickened at the thought. . . . My body craved death, it was so sickened by the certainty that my mind understood. But there was no other way. There was no other way I knew of. How else could I conquer life? How else but this constant brutish struggle?

Sighing, I turned once again to the sea.

I forced myself to step back into the water. I shuddered with the cold, with exhaustion, with a vertigo of the soul that leapt out to the mad vertigo of the ocean; I gave one backward forlorn half-hopeful glance to the lighthouse. . . . I would submit to what I knew; I could perform in no other way; if there were other clarities, other strategies of triumph, they belong to the future, and I had no acquaintance with them; and anyway I have never minded Death.

II *Forbidden Testimonies*

What she did never exactly mirrored
what she was. . . .
    —overheard in conversation

Forbidden
Testimony

Because I could not know
how love shook you
more violent than my own cries
I did not know our marriage—
swimming in air
unwitnessed.

The rooftops shone with sun
and tar.
Silence up here. City noises.
My voice in a scream
I had never heard before.

I the 'fourteen-year-old girl'
you the 'thirty-seven-year-old man
     of no fixed address'
I tell you in this newer pain
how I did not know
at the instant of breakage—
how could I?

knowing only what screamed and flew apart

In our marriage of three minutes
terror performs over and over
a tumbling act
a nine-story fall to the street.
A failure of love.
An error.

An Age of Miracles

He walked to the window
stared down twenty stories to the street
gaseous and dizzy as a swamp
not visible at this height
but there had been a street down there
and he knew

It came with the apartment
and the guarded foyers and halls
and the doorman
holstered
beneath the uniform
the television split-screening
front and rear entrances

He knew it was all there
and he was here twenty stories above
the unsettled swamp-mist
he knew the trucks bound for the bridge
were still passing near
he could feel them rumbling
in the soles of his feet
so he knew

the floor he walked on
was someone's ceiling
and it was all normal tonight
and countable
a two-year lease because
a desirable
with full view of
river-
a five-by-three balcony though the door is
$200 deposit
fully carpeted
self-defrosting refriger-
the balcony door is stuck but

He can stare twenty stories down
from the windowsill
watching the swamp smokes curl and thin
and the swamp lapping at the base
and the unpaid-for miracle
one inch at a time

"After Twelve Years of
Traveling Constantly. . . ."

because it was mute
drawing me out
the land drawing me
the sea drawing me out of myself

because constant movement
works a miracle of erosion
on the face: wiped clean
features back to zero

I could have no children at this pace
my body gone sterile with the rapid
pace of the aircraft that carried me away
any point on the map was a joy
to leave

cruder and cruder
the continents
perfect blanks of color
harsh blows of unimagined mornings
working backward to the single morning
the original unhuman morning

I kept traveling because
I could not stop
changing with the continents
the stopovers in predawn airports
flowing with the pace of days
always unimagined
always the same day

everything open! original!
after twelve years of travel
constant erosion of foreign winds
I have no face   no single name
I am anyone
any landscape
any momentum

Breaking
and Entering

One of us touched the door and it swung open.

Slowly, we went inside,
Knowing better, we went inside.

The kitchen was darkened,
the light we'd left on in the hallway was out.
Downstairs, no sign of disorder.
Knowing better, we went upstairs.
If I had tried to caution you, you would have pulled away,
eager, anxious, needing to see—
and there in the bedroom
the acted-out drama, there
bureau drawers yanked out, overturned, thrown,
a skid mark on one wall—
our clothes tumbled together—
twisted, kicked, someone's fury run to earth.
On the doorframe there is a smear of blood.

Later, we will discover the smashed window in the basement;
the drops of a stranger's blood.
He must have been very small, the police said,
to crawl through there.
Later, slowly, as if shy of knowledge,
we discover things missing:
my wristwatch, a small typewriter,
a tarnished silver vase.
We are slowed-down, stupefied.
We want none of our possessions back,
we don't care what else has been stolen,
yet we talk about it constantly:
the mess! the surprise!

Later, we will transform it into an anecdote.
We will say, *One of us touched the door and it swung open.* . . .
knowing no way to explain the stupor, the despair,
the premonition of theft to come.

The Fear of
Going Blind

there will be the clerkish questions
with their multiple tiers
the analysis of fine-meshed gears and wheels
    that have failed now, curiously

where are you hiding, crouched
inside your head?

and the hands in pairs gloved with the dark
the framing of my invisible face
the examination of the little bronze wheels
of my eyes *where are you hiding*
where have you retreated
why did you believe you could escape us?

Two Insomniacs

if one rises to stare out a window
the other feels the tugging, the draft of air
if one shuts his eyes
the other feels the leap of a half-vision
that does not take hold

between them a few miles
the chopped-up ridges of a city
others' dreams that whine
like nighttime sirens

this is what they wanted
this is what the legends promised them
and if one telephones the other, the ringing
will anger the night and then subside
to nothing: they will both listen then to nothing
because this is what they wanted
and this is what they got

An American Tradition

Returning gifts!

At the K-Mart in Marietta, Georgia,
the morning after Christmas morning,
there they wait, a small crowd,
waiting for the doors to open at ten.
Some carry bulky cardboard boxes: Mixmasters,
electric football games, chenille bedspreads.
Others grip paper bags into which gifts have been stuffed,
price tags still attached.

Excitement as ten o'clock nears!
By now the outer doors are opened;
they advance into the foyer, happily,
where vending machines offer
rubber lizards, 5-Minit Photos, and popcorn
kept fresh by yellow lights.
They wait.

But someone is not patient, someone is muttering—
no, it is a couple—
a woman in a fur-lined parka, her husband in his shirtsleeves—
You think you're so superior— *You want to make me crawl*—
Suddenly she is crying.
Suddenly she is elbowing her way back out, out
of the jammed-in pack, suddenly her face is contorted,
she is one of them, but a stranger.
What rage, what bitterness!—
this woman sensing a gift
she cannot return.

Coast Guard
Rescue Maneuvers

upon the raked beach is the shadow
its propellers are slow-spinning
slow, very slow, roaring and slow
slow-pumping like great crude swords
or like the ceiling fans of the past:
slow enough for the eye

on the lake, an open boat
men miniature but evidently real
and above them now the slow helicopter
vibration of its roar
the small tamed waves shudder
the plate glass window shudders
where the woman stands
staring
her brain registers the throb of the motor
the men are too small
to be seen

the Coast Guard helicopter is white
with red trim
navy blue insignia
ropes—men—arms—slow propellers—slow-
roaring, the vibrations merge
into the day's waves
the beach's wavelike strands of sand
baked hard by the sun

       one day she hurried down to the beach
       running plunging down the long lawn's drop
       three in the afternoon, was it?
       still in her bedroom slippers
       but they were too far away
       moving slowly downstream
       boat and helicopter and roaring
       the great propellers turning and the roar
       easing downstream and away
       fading into the ordinary wash of waves
       ordinary panting of her breath

Lovers

The telephone rings again.
She answers it,
again.
Again the hostility of his silence and again
she hangs up, panicked.

Again it rings,
Her hand reaches out.
Yes? Hello? What do you want?
Why are you—
He is silent, he waits.

If she leaves the apartment the telephone will ring
ring and ring
no one to count how many times—
twenty-eight, twenty-nine, thirty—
the door slammed shut against the ringing
which finally stops

      and starts again
an hour or a week later.

She wonders if he telephones while she is away.
She wonders if he stands somewhere,
ready to pitch forward into her silence.
She wonders—why does he love her, so strangely?
Is she a woman he has touched?

In her wondering he advances, he attacks.
He withdraws.
Sometimes when she lifts the receiver she hears nothing—
not even his silence.
She then replaces the receiver slowly,
wonder filling her like a god.

A Heroine
Without a Story

it must be the middle of the story
the story must already have begun

in the alleyway behind Metropolitan Five & Dime
she stumbles, half-undressed
the blue dress very short
her thighs very thin
ankles ghastly-white but cute
shoes with brave chunky heels
exactly in the style of this season's
heroines

why is her dress unzipped?
six inches of pale freckled backbone there
no one to notice, a loss
except the black parking attendant
who looks away quickly
he is safe in his little cabin
as she stumbles through the alley
pauses by the garbage bin
behind Detrow's Office Supplies
now it is raining, now she holds the bag of potato chips
close to her chin
she is eating, childlike, vague and hungry
hand-over-hand eating potato chips
in the rain
now behind Mayfair Shoes
and the black attendant looks away,
quickly

one of the blue bows hangs untied
she turns, her long straight hair
blond like a heroine's
she turns with a baffled frown
looking for the audience
but there is no one
the parking attendant looks away
a final time

he will not be questioned
nothing will happen
in ten minutes he will look back
cautious
the alley will be empty
nobody will be questioned
nothing will happen

what she did, what she was—
no one witnessed

Lies Lovingly Told

Every man adores
the woman who adores
    the Fascist:
she the destroyer of his children
she who ravages his wife's sleep

her Evil cannot be marred by tears
nor has she squint lines at the corners of those marvelous Eyes
her name cannot be sounded as a diminutive, like his and ours,
and she is poster-poreless

ah, she adores his adoring her!

—and she is never revised—
sprung full from his loins
in the poetry of late childhood

—she must never be revised—

Every man adores
the woman who cracks and dies cleanly
who is buried by strangers
whose death is none of his business.

To a Victim

Are you required to lie with them to prove
how pale you are, and innocent?
Are you to be picked clean?
Are you resisting arrest when the streets expand
    to hide you?

In the embrace of the unappeasable lovers
the universe contracts to a single cry.

Are you guilty, to hear it?

Are you the counter of the Void, that hordes must
    tumble into you?
Let them tear at the flesh of their own wives.
Let them scream at the daylight as it darkens about them.
Let them write angry letters to the Government—
    they haven't been loved enough, there has been some crime!

In the end, let them bear false witness.
You cannot make them gods: you must be punished.

A Friend Moving
Out of Our Lives

Back from the dark side of the earth
our friend has come to visit with us, for a few days—
his face will not break, composed to earnest
conversation, the meeting of eyes that are never
    pleading
for any kind of special love

He looks leaner than we remember
there is something haggard about his young face
and he begins to speak of "another year away"
another year is all that is needed

But:
the innocence is weary, the ironies of old friends
stifled at half-smiles
he is carrying to that other continent
the sorrow of thirty years locked
in the same skeleton, behind the same
    unhating American face
where so much hate has boiled, crazily—
someday his face will darken with it

Demanding *Why, why?*

Why has no one taught him to love properly?—
why has no one scolded him into shape?—
why the carnal kingdom of husbands and wives,
    a distant dark continent he cannot enter?

Yes, the normal smile at such questions
it is part of being "normal," to smile at such questions
smiling constantly with small pitying smiles
knowing the rules
the absolute limits

He is baffled by his numerous loves
as by wasps darting
about his innocent head
so many loves!—and so vaporous, so forgettable!
he cannot get them into one room, into one face
    that might be memorized
he does not know that the rules of the game declare:
two persons, two sexes, a house and lot and forms
to fill out for the Government, proof of
    good citizenship
proof that the years can pass in careful handfuls
in the daylight of one side
of the moving earth

The Survivor

The newsagent's *Evening Standards* were being delivered.
The London sky, close about our heads, had gone invisible.
We clasped hands, we embraced, we parted.

Now, your death is an outrage
distorted by quarreling details—
the testimonies of wife, friends,
friends of friends, the muted display
of life in old enemies—
Now only the embrace is real,
the ghost-hand tugging at my own.

Your death can be survived. It must.
But what was sloughed off, what is voiceless now—
lost to your extravagant laughter—
what is denied your jokes—the reckless blotch
of your innocent feuds—

> The survivor stammers.
> He knows too much.

The terror of which no one speaks is not death.
It is not pain, not even the surprise of pain.
'Not the height but the sudden drop'—
as Nietzsche knew, who lived then
to survive himself.

In the Street

inhabiting these costumes with their holy used look
prowling the sidewalks, heads heavy as if bewigged,
the children are grown tall
barefoot or sandaled or in military boots to the knee

no bat-shaped wedges fly between inhalation and exhalation
no thoughts slash the seamless fabric
    of the perpetual day

all is silence inside them

in the street are lost the maps of a weekend
lost the paragraphing of the lives
lost the words that—
the words that —

in such a din of silence
the self is only syntactical
the legs only maneuver to keep from falling

Spaces

you seize my wrist
and in the mad leap of our eyes
is that silence

the air buoying our words
is heavy with silence
spaces of silence before and after
the breathed words
unknowable
as the spaces between heartbeats
between the frail creatures of our nerves
strung like a second skeleton
through the body

this morning on the riverbank, high
about the choppy river
a man was shouting into space
into a sky of cold blue layers
a man shouting at a child or a dog
or at no one
and after the last fury of sound
came his stunned silence
when words gave out

I could not move away
but felt how we were one
strangers in that instant of silence
exhausted with noise
we must fall silent, as exhausted
with love we lie back separate
separated

but the silence buoys us up
the spaces where we cannot lie
buoy us up, undrowned
when the love-shouts fade into spaces
when the breathing-spaces fade
into spaces

Lorelei

Out of a rain-green field
I approached you
you saw nothing
you felt fear

Out of a boy-sized dream
I walked head-on
into your embrace
your agitation was all body
the dream steepened
and you died

The time you left home
to spend a few weeks alone
in a shanty so cold you couldn't undress
but lay in sleep-stale clothes
it was I outside the rusted screen
a foot from your head
it was I drawing a fingernail
across the screen, lightly,
to wake you in terror

Though now you never sleep alone
though your wife is warm, curled
against you
the sudden tension of her sleep
the quickened breathing
shows how I liquify inside her
beat by beat
filling out inside her
with her consent

"But I Love. . . ."

When you are being pursued
you cannot think of anything else.
These autumnal landscapes—the Lake Michigan shore—
turn neutral as the blurred backgrounds
of photographs.

Useless, the labor of unloving
you beg him to begin.
Useless, your explanations.
He does not listen.
Yes, he listens, but smiles patiently.
Because he pursues you he is defined to himself
as one who pursues you
as one in constant bitter pursuit
as one who does not listen or who listens
but smiles patiently.

Friendly as ever, your mirrored face
is innocent.
No magic there.
Only a look of terror
that will surely pass.
Surely, if you explain once again. . . .

You protest that you are innocent.
There is no magic to you.
Yes, but he too is innocent and will protest.
He too is flesh and loves yours.
You protest, "This must be a misunderstanding. . . ."
Yes, but the misunderstanding is part of the struggle.
And, in any case, the misunderstanding is all
the two of you share,
and is his life.

Blizzard

There are small stinging sand-
sized deaths
breaking on the heat
of the surface
of the skin

smiles melting in a miracle
of flesh and wind

> *What are the words we use—*
> *What are the names we call each other—*
> *In this snowstorm we cannot hear*

Such words as are air
are blown into a galaxy
into pupils of white-blind eyes
that flash and withdraw and reassemble
everywhere about us

> *—cannot hear each other—*

Snowflakes like insects swollen
with white blood
shift the afternoon harshly to night
as the two of us struggle
heads bowed
lungs shallow
the darkness alive with slashing blasts
the wind hammering with its voice
this familiar landscape surrendered
to the enemy
to the fine-ground sleeping potion
that encrusts our eyelashes
and melts stinging against our flesh

> *What words we use, what names—*
> *What words by which we compose ourselves?*

Sinners in the Hand
of a Righteous God

Newly brittle, the snow's crust resists our weight.
Our booted heels can hardly crack it.
And what of the earth we must imagine now,
     miles and years into winter?
Frozen hard as moon rock.

Nothing has changed, or everything.

The wind is as insolent, the sky as razorish a blue.
The same people in the same overcoats are walking
     muffled, heads bowed into the wind.

Is it winter that burdens them, or their innocence?

We, having sinned, stride through the freezing afternoon.
Our eyes burn with tears, but only from the river's wind.
Our guilty smiles shade into steam.

Sinners may be cleansed pure as snow,
     by snow.
No God abides in this landscape but the landscape:
Brittle the crust, perfection in each footprint.

Flight

Christmas morning. Glowing-white sands.
High clouds speeding toward noon,
like our car.
We leap into focus only
when fear subsides.

Above unreadable swamps hover wide-winged hawks
and below are crook-necked white birds,
nameless.
Here are original things.
Flaming in the perpetual sun are flamingos:
they glide like sleepwalkers, on pencil-thin legs,
then squawk themselves awake.
We awake, and drive away.

BOMBING RAIDS RESUMED—
a glimpsed unpaid-for headline,
a Miami newspaper.
We drive away in a greater hurry now
to noon at Alapha Key, from there
to Naples, on the Gulf, from there to
macaws bright as painted birds, trained
by prison inmates to perform:
to paint, play poker, to ride bird-sized bicycles,
to keep to their cross-staved perches, unchained.
They shriek melodramatically,
but without rage.

In the roadside restaurants are waitresses with stiff stacked hair
and patient, creased faces, working on Christmas Day.
Our mothers' ages, they hurry from tables to kitchen to tables
smiling endlessly, without focus,
as we drive away into a glowering sky.
It is all right, it will transform itself in the end.
But the gasoline is high-octane and propels us away—
CASUALTIES SOAR ON BOTH SIDES—
to the edge of the hard-packed sand
where droves of sandpipers flit, in fluid darts,
in one direction and then suddenly in another,
reversing themselves in communal magic.
Our heads are thunderous with surf
and nowhere left to go.

Seizure

and you are gone

outside the window sparrows cascade upward
your neighbor, in an old jacket, is trudging to the river
where the sun flies off the banked-up ice
and the spicy-green stinging-green heads of mallards
and behind you the house is right-angled, perfect
as constructed things can be perfect

sunlight broken by windowpanes falls slantwise
in your seizure
light manic pounding that is not a metaphor
at the center of your body
the body not a metaphor
and breath goes shallow, swift, chopping with cunning
to get you through
not a metaphor for breath but breath
breath itself needing to be intelligent

outside, there is breathing
it is all breathing calmly
the turbulence of the birds is their breathing
their souls emerge like that, in spurts of noise
the constant bobbing of the ducks, dipping
the waves caressing them roughly
out where the half-dozen yards of raw ice
breathes into the river

thoughts rise in you in quick darts
the thoughts you recall from the last seizure
needing to stand like this, paralyzed,
in a timeless time
where the center of your body is unfriendly
and you need to think
dying now in a house of right-angled perfections
a borrowed celebration of sunshine and birds
how good, how ordinary—

take it as a gift

but the body sweats with panic
can't believe death is so easy
can't believe it is always yourself
surrendered to that breathing

III *The Child-Martyr*

The Child-Martyr

Not white-faced, exactly, but sour-cream-colored, a vicious color, so that his eyes—heavily outlined in black—and his insipid mouth—salmon-rosy— were exaggerated. The contortions of the mouth were exaggerated too. It must have been a mistake, but the parted lips revealed no teeth, only that absurd leadish black.

In glassy perfection, around him, were an aquatic blue and rosy-beige and a yellow too sullen with browns to represent sunshine, and of course a repetition of the unearthly white of his face. And the black. In the usual winter drizzle all colors looked sullen. But when the Ideal slipped into position behind the Real all went vivid, and for an instant his original martyrdom was evoked in that thrill of ecstatic pain: only the too-thick black panels between the pieces of glass reminded one of earth, of weighty metals.

In the melodrama of an audience's pity (a small audience—usually women, usually old women) the grimace tightened; the slits of eyes seemed to shriek. It had been a habit, a long habit. It must have been a dream in the mind of whoever had put the window together. . . . One morning, however, the Child-Martyr allowed the grimace to twitch only on the right side of his mouth, the left remaining frozen. Did anyone notice. . . ? And one day he allowed the lips' natural desire to scream in church an inch or two of freedom, only two-dimensional, only visual: *a nasty grin.*

No more than three feet high, the Child-Martyr enjoyed a certain magnification because of an accident in the structure of the building. Located near the back pews, his window faced out on pavement; some of the other windows had become shaded, over the years, by oaks. So he enjoyed more sunshine. And the odor of damp and piety aided him because a child was out of place in this setting, one's sympathies were evoked at once . . . it was like discovering the skeleton of a kitten in an old cellar, with an earthen floor.

Though it was clear from the very first that the Child-Martyr was shifting inside the brute lead outlines, no one dared notice. There was a tradition of tear droplets, a tradition of stigmata, bloodstains and streaks exactly the color of real blood and drying even to the color of real blood. But the Child-Martyr was too young for tradition, or too stunted in his growth—his legs had been hurriedly and clumsily fashioned, tucked out of sight—for this alone he would never forgive the artisan who had pieced him together! He was poised up there, as if ready to spring. Fully awake and yet pretending to be asleep, but not with the grace of a respectful pretense, with a deliberately coarse pretense . . . an insult to his worshipers.

Of course they were not "his" alone; they rotated their worship from day to day, and on special private occasions, on occasions that involved tears and a mute terrible shaking of the head, they went to special windows, often to his. He did not mind sharing them. As time passed he longed to be less attractive, he did not at all mind the days no one prayed to him. . . . But it wasn't until he began to stare rudely at them through his black-edged eyes that he discovered a way of driving some away. Cunning, sly, furious in that sourish-white face, he discovered at the same time a centuries-old delight, slumbering in him.

Ah, the virginal dreamy stupidity of cold glass! He wanted music, he wanted more space. He began to murmur, to groan. A gutteral murmur back in the throat, a mockery of chaste agony . . . a mockery of the chastity that always stared up at him, out of others' eyes. *Who are you worshiping. . . ? Is this only a mirror?* —He sensed, from the immediate response, the cringing, the bewilderment, the fear, the tics —he sensed, in triumph, in a joy he had not felt since the original martyrdom, that he was correct in that diagnosis. *All along he had been a mirror.* And now he was coming alive to protest the stupidity of his makers, his worshipers, his importance, his amateurishly assorted features, his own ordeal. That ordeal had been pleasurable, but this, in glass, in the dank cellarish air, this was a lie. —A low gutteral moan. Bestial and intelligent. Groping to become audible. Inquisitive. *Am I. . . ? Am I becoming one of you. . . ? Language instead of glass, music instead of mute babyish screams. . . ?*

For centuries he, like the others on the side walls, stared slantwise to the altar . . . out of the corner of their souls they envied that position, the fullest whining triumphant martyrdom . . . in gold, in emeralds and diamonds and paste-pale exquisite flesh . . . a halo that shone without fear of being comic. Centuries of envy and silence. Now the Child-Martyr's low chuckle shattered those centuries. Someone was to write incoherently of him, scribbling down words as if to dispel the original chaos: *Evidently before the assumption of one's role in history, evidently before, evidently all the possibilities are in the seed (seeds?), evidently . . . yes but how to . . . how to unhook (unlock?) them without, with, without causing tidal waves and earthquakes, without . . . with full respect for one's ancestors and the Inquisition in the Marketplace. . . .* But he ripped all this up. He prayed to the Child-Martyr to be delivered of his own madness. And yet again he found himself writing: *. . . before the beginning of history itself, before it, before it pieces the shards together . . .* But what? What came before? What was it, where did it go, why is it lost, why is it now a nasty gap-mouthed grin? He ripped the pages up, prayed elsewhere with his rosary wrapped so tightly about his knuckles that the flesh showed the marks of the smooth black beads.

Am I. . . ? Am I becoming human. . . ?

Am I becoming God. . . ?

God awakening in him made him childish and vicious and lopsided in his grinning—naturally he must mock, after such an eternity of fraudulent suffering! Whose fault is it, sneers the Child-Martyr, who invented all this martyrdom? Rolling his eyes back in his head he caught sight one day of the insipid halo floating three or four inches above him, in utter sky-blue virginity, and for an instant he wondered—with the terrible clarity of the child—if, all along, someone had been mocking him anyway. But the instant passed. *No, too good to have been true!* And the ironies accumulate, the insulting histrionic groans move toward language.   *—nearly audible?*

He has a dread of the immediate future: of whispers that grow to exclamations and public prayers and public adorations, of a new excited worship of that old fraudulent martyrdom. Famous, must he become famous and martyred once again, so that no one will hear the sly innuendos in the moans, no one will smash the mirror and free him? Another possibility, which terrifies him even more, is that they will seize upon the parody and stumble away with it, stunned and giggling with it, and the original pain—so real, so exquisite!—will be totally lost.

Still, he writhes into life. Evidently it is his fate.

the blood-smear across the knuckles:
painless, inexplicable.
once you discover it pain will begin,
in miniature.
never will you learn what caused it.
you forget it.

the telephone answered on the twelfth ring:
silence without breath, cunning, stark.
and then he hangs up.
and you stand there, alone.
then you forget.

and your father's inexplicable visit:
two days' notice, a ten-hour reckless drive.
rains, 80 mph winds, bad luck all the way,
traffic backed up, a broken windshield wiper,
and no stopping him.

clumsy handshakes.
How are—?
You seem—!
How good to —!
How long will—?
he must leave in the morning,
must get back.
a gas station two blocks away repairs the wiper.

did he sense death,
and so he raced to us?
did he already guess at his death
behind those nervous fond smiles,
the tumult of memories he had to bear?

nothing we know can explain his visit,
or the new, strange way he moved among us—
touching us, squeezing our arms, smiling.
the visit was an excuse.
the words that surrounded our touching were an excuse.
inexplicable, that the language we invent may be a means
to get us closer, to allow us to touch one another,
and then to back away.

In Case of
Accidental Death

Someone's sinewy hands somewhere fail.
Sweat-slick, the wheel spins.
The wheels spin.
A guard railing buckles and explodes.

Spun, reeling
the confined air dense with an explosion of thought—
too late, too late!
a premature separation—

Plans for a cosmic death
become only local.
Noisy, end-over-end,
a car's graceless bulk
an odor of gasoline.

In America things often occur
prematurely.

Useless, a door swings open—

But perhaps there will be ditchwater
and spiky tart-smelling weeds
and overhead a heavy airliner
with passengers marveling
at the landscape
and an unswervable destination.

> What plans?
> what promise?
> it is here
> it is somehow good
>
> being local is also a tradition
> in this country

Promiscuity

Erthe upon erthe is wonderly wrought
Erthe upon erthe hath worship of nought. . . .
                    —medieval poem

 * No choice.

 * A slow circling parade, shuffling
   of miscellaneous feet. Imperfect anatomies
   to mock some perfect destiny.
   They keep glancing from side to side,
   in envy.

 * Each time the camera advanced
   smiles appeared.

 * On Fridays the Discount Foods is open 'til 9.
   Like the decks of a sickened ship
   the aisles are awash with shapes—
   crates half-unpacked,
   pyramids of cans,
   women pushing shopping carts
   balky as wire animals.
   Children run free, freely in the aisles,
   unlabeled.

 * Someone's dog begins to bark.
   A mile away, another dog barks.
   Out of wild weedy ditches the wild dogs
   stammer and howl.
   Ice forms between their toes.
   On a distant city street another dog
   lifts its muzzle to wail.
   We wake at the same moment
   in the same bed.

* It looked like a mountain,
  it even had jagged peaks.
  But by June it began to thaw.
  By August, even the rivulets in our backyards
  had dried.
  We did not drown.
  We do not miss the drama
  of the jagged peaks.

What Has Not Been Lost in the
Deserts of North America?

Scraps of happiness flutter with the black picnic flies.
Bullet-riddled signs fall too swiftly: *Beware of. Hazard.*
On a small mountain rocks arranged to spell out—
But the road swerves away and the rocks have rolled downhill
and wobbling at 70 mph is a cyclist heading West with us—
        skin near-blackened, iridescent helmet,
        caution of head and shoulders and torso.

What do we care of distant evolved mountains visited only once?
Of photographs that show us not as we live
but as we rear back in panic,
to be photographed?
History cannot record the foreground.
Hazard. Slow. Runaway Lane 40 mph. Exit. Clearance 16'6".
Resume Speed.

Winds at all windows rush upon us
and what is sucked out one window
flies back in another—
sun-scorched, tasting of salt.

Midday

When Love fails loves fail.
The declension is almost musical.

Being after being falls back—
separate, whole. Strangers.
Moons become chunks of unreflecting rock.

How our friends' faces are exposed!
Their souls exposed, strangers!
They were separate and whole long before we lived.
They were children on distant coasts, in walled
villages in Europe.

As Love fails the backgrounds of blurred shots
rise to prominence.
The world shifts to midday.
Like stained glass it awakens to midday.

When Love fails loves fail
waking us to the equilibrium of loss.
The midday shifts back inside us.

We are awakened: we wake.

Closure

You pursued me as if this were not a game
of mid-life
as if your flesh had tricked you
the eyes stricken white-rimmed with dread
for what you forced of us.

Our mouths together, a communion of wounds.
In all such blood there is anonymous life.

The roads we drove along, aimlessly,
through one winter and spring,
are not now crumpled or barricaded—but are exactly the same.
Even the median's ravaged thistles are the same.

The rising of certain loves is—
The dying of certain loves—

When agony becomes anonymous it is perfection.

Being Faithful

There are faceless mouths beneath our feet,
sucking-sighing
at the agitated edge of the continent, at noon.
How bright the sun is, how monstrous!
Small shifting channels in the sand
have the look of rivers
between tragic shores.
Our bare feet shy away
from the untidy shells,
our sunburnt bodies cringe
at the invisible nudges. . . .
We know we have been this way before:
a man walking ahead of a woman,
squinting in the spray, the wind,
one walking into the footprints of the other.

The third night in a row, a cigarette burn
on the bedcovers!—the same odor of mildew
and insecticide!
Hundreds of miles have passed.
Hundreds of cows have slept beneath pine trees.
Formality? Perfection?
In the morning there will be a road pot-holed and slanted,
ahead, in the mist, a truck heavy with logs
will strain uphill at 20 miles per hour.
We must overtake the truck, we must rear over the hill.
All this must happen
again.

Each night on the highway
cars rush past, appearing to gain speed
as they approach.
Unsleeping, I watch for hours.
Drivers must prepare all their lives
for certain short lunges
past darkened farmhouses, where a girl watches,
faithful to them.
They appear, they gain speed, they rush transformed
into the rush of wheels, the scan of headlights,
the wind.
Then the sudden fading-away
the highway empty again
abstract
unimagined.

Fireflies

palpitations come to life
teasing
miniature mocking egos

like flirtations they are,
though said to be alive
and singular
as nerve-twitches
gone placid at last—
calming the mind
because there is no pattern
in their sudden bodies
and the deaths of their bodies

Are they sweetened, like us,
by touches scant
as tongue-tips?
they tease the eye outward
to what is not human but knowable
and then not knowable
and not a pattern
not a thought
not singular

Mourning and Melancholia:
In Memory of Sylvia Plath

Ceaseless
and raw beneath the eyelids
visions work, unsleeping.

A dream rears backward, and a dream
works upward to the eye.
The eye-muscles cannot resist.
Exhausted with dreams they move
into focus, again

And then wake: a morning's weather
a noise of undreamt distance
where strangers accelerate
powerful machines.

Ceaseless the noise, the strangers—
Readying for enormities, we are anchored hard
unpitiable.
We persist in our Being.
We are never known.

Approaching the
Speed of Light

>   . . . it is not we who play with words,
> but the nature of language plays
> with us.
>
> —Heidegger

no one to step forward
no handshake
no embrace
no one to cry *We've been waiting—*

brute expanses only
skies of any color, any texture
unpredictable
perfect
strangers everywhere
worlds that don't know us

and cannot imagine us
cannot name us
lying beyond our imaginations as we beyond theirs
innocent and murderous of pride
—a muddy twilight in West Virginia
—a field of ravaged cornstalks
—the ghastly Exxon sign rearing in the night

space contracts
        and expands
we sense ourselves born again with each mile
springing effortlessly into life
forgetting what we learn
moving gravely, carefully
memorizing the terrain as it flies beneath us
forgetting it again
and being forgotten

After the Storm

the river is rising three inches an hour
   three-and-a-half inches an hour

The Coast Guard is urging everyone to—
Blankets and coffee at the Armory—
Evacuation crews have asked us to warn—

when the emergency bulletins are silenced
all is wind-rocking wind-moaning
but silent
a sanity in the crash of the waves
a few hundred feet away

the house is not a ship
yet the walls strain to crack
heaved by air like an ocean
snowflakes are drummed into rain
rumors of apocalyptic beasts

so sleepless a world demands embraces!

that rhythm of hollows and starts
will not build to madness:
the wind will die at 5:30 A.M.
the sleepless will arise
into an ordinary day

        Now it is dawn.
        Rain-chilled, ugly.
        Logs and broken things jammed in the piling.
        Now daylight, now nearing noon.
        Where is the God of that landscape?
        Our radio turned off, we cannot hear
        anyone weeping, or the shouts of the elderly
        resisting help.
        Now it is noon in the storm's after-quake.
        Puddles ripple from east to west, a foot deep.
        Now it is noon in a planet of debris
        viewed from a dustless moon.
        Who can weep bitterly at the God of that landscape?
        Who can weep bitterly at what was betrayed?

While We Slept. . . .

         . . . snow piled without effort
blown through the windows' rusty screens, drifting
     thinly on the porch
silences fell while we slept

moths in last night's warm lamplight
stilled now in these dunes
           of white silence
as we slept
in the wise vacuum of those
who desire sorrow without the effort
     of tears

         . . . the sleeping secret in us
embryo-breathing that breathes us
snow-freshened air in its own rhythms, breathing
     into us who sleep, breathing
us as we sleep

         . . . the blankets, already damp, turned heavy
with the long night
the cabin's low ceiling pressed nearer
cobwebs teasing our faces
     while we slept
hoping to survive this spell
hoping for a morning's strident anger
shouting *No! no!*
       we are too young for this—
       always too young for this—

there is a place for death and a place for love
a place where finally a sky will emerge damply-blue
there are birds in the evergreen bushes—
already the new snow is tracked—
and sleep has no wisdom
great as daylight.

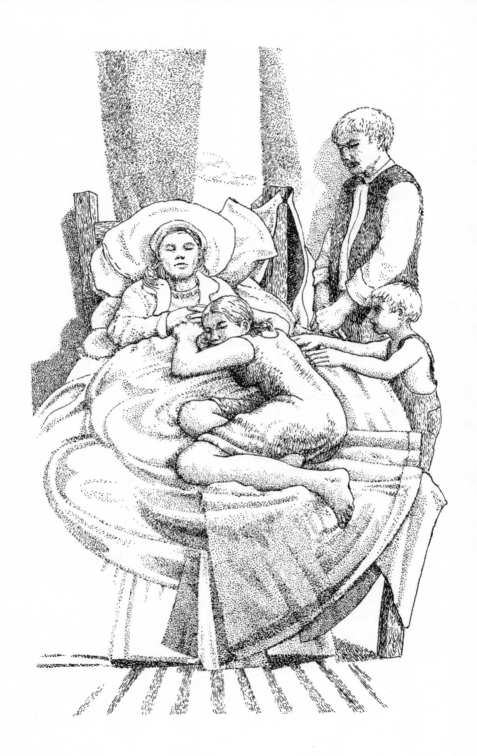

The Forgiveness
of Sins

The dying embrace us
and it is not necessary to confess
how, squirming in one embrace,
someone yearns crazily for another
how, that day downtown,
someone ducked into a drugstore
to avoid someone else

the blue-rinsed hair, the day-old Easter orchid
in its plastic vial!

The dying embrace us
their shiny-skinned fingers are forgiving
always an odor of soapy warmth
above the hospital sheets
Someone will always be dying
someone will always be forgiven

Is it necessary to confess
how, weeping in one embrace,
someone is already wiping tears away
already walking toward the car?

Dying, they know these ordinary facts.
They love, they forgive.
They instruct.

London Winter

clocked today at two-fifteen
the dusk of this northerly city
inches backward to noon
slow
reversing of an old miracle

what looks like concrete opens
cracks in the pavement sprawl
as the soft cores push
free

          and free
the risk of daylight gone
the risk of complex light gone
under strings of electricity

now the underside of the city breathes
in traffic-slow rhythms
a strange careless
weightless
breath in the heavy-
moving forms

as the souls of hard things push
shapeless
free of their names
and sprawl
undoing us back to noon to morning
to dawn

20.26 Knots

pock-marked and heaving
resilient as a mad mind
the waves of the visible ocean
make war upon us

we avoid the ship's open decks
fearing the open water
the waves heaped up meanly and meanly falling back
to sea

groggily in swaying crowds
we walk and re-walk the carpeted closed floors
tilting, gone muscleless
with no destination beyond the ship's mapped floors ,
our minds like clocks leaping forward
an hour to the east
each midnight

in the Atlantic the wind is many-branched
a chanting of watery pits and graves
shouting us down and back
into burrows
braced against the pitch
the giant vibrating breath
of the famous ship

the waves out here are not blue but blackened
water reflecting any known sky

uncoordinated are the swells
undecipherable the ship's instruments
we burrow inward, down
beneath the heaving lines of latitude
to the ship's warmed center
hands pressed over ears
someone engineers us rockily
through the original sea

In Air

the cellar rises
into daylight

earth hard-packed
from decades of feet
chunks of coal
scattered
stiffened paint rags
rivulets worn in the soil from a hose
    drooping from the old hand-washer

the cistern is dry
dried in a permanent August
if anything crawls in now it will not drown
will not be maneuvered out
with a broom and a shovel
carried carefully away for burial

there are old secrets
when houses are razed
and the explosion of their dust lifts
like the dust of those famous
photographed bombs

rust-flecked cobwebs are idle in air
and will not brush against our faces
hack-saw blades lay severed with rust
the earth and its undigested things
glare in daylight
we hoped no one outside the family
would ever see

and there finally beneath an upended crate
by the coal bin
there lies the old ax-handle
the blade is missing
did it fly off into space?
is it embedded somewhere in air?

Music

November: dust is wetted and leaves
safe now from fire. The river's wind is
noisy today. Yesterday someone said to me,
'Part of every cell is immortal—nothing dies.'

Trees are blown apart at their tops
the skeletons emerge frightened
boisterous windy bodies clutch at them
in a wailing that must be music
we cannot understand. . . .
Yet nothing dies.
I think of dinosaurs and 'saber-toothed
tigers' and a shabby unconvincing herd
penned in museums for children
yawning through Saturday afternoons.
I think of the music
I can think of.
This is another music, unlearnable.
Nothing dies but remains in the sleepy eyes
of cats, or in the protoplasm of plants
or shrill with this shouting
of November.

A Vision

there was nothing
until a junk-yard vast as a kingdom
tossed up light:
a galaxy of particles, glittering
one single explosion
broken
into bits

one glow of light
pin-pricked
like a fly's miracle
of an eye

then there was nothing again
except the sign of Highway 98
dull-gleaming metal
the aftermath of a vision

IV *The Fabulous Beasts*

Fabulous Beast

My fingers are dirty with newsprint.
It sticks beneath the nails, in the eyelashes,
    it is smudged against the eye's white.
It is smeared on walls—shapes of hands dragging down.

Who is in those bombers, photographed grainily from shore?
Who is scrambling for cover inside a thatched hut?
It is 1939, it is Northern Africa. It is 1968.
No: it is tonight's paper.
It is a yellowed page fluttering in the wind.

Who was that, scrambling for cover?

Who is preparing the newspaper today, who is preparing
    tomorrow's lay-out?
Who is being photographed?
Ditches. Broad nameless roads. On stretchers, in stockades,
    in a tangle of mud and vines squeezed between advertisements.

Who is stooping now to drag the newsprint in?

There are new bombers, there are new autumn cars,
always new photographs, new captions.
Decades of pages flutter with disaster and routine.
Who is yawning, typing up forms?
Who is photographed, blinking in the glare,
    awaking in the newsprint on p. 29-A,
    beside this week's discount sale?

    A huge creature, its outer membrane not yet congealed,
stirs no more than a flame as you enter.

Wooded Forms

a leafbeat
an interior vertigo
springs to us from the ring-
upon-ring of their spine
their memories imprinted in pulp
wooden flesh fragrant at the core
the soul fluid in surrender
to chain-saw
or sun

perfect in possession
of a form
grown of earth in leaps
straining to its farthest tendrils'
possession of dirt and air
measurable cubic yards

their kind of flesh leaps
through history
in one place
singular
multiplied endlessly

      ours strains to see
      our desperation is to see
      imagining our own forms
      blood-netted air
      thrown across the continent
      wild and tamed and again
      ring upon ring of our memories
      savage and again
      in newer rhythms
      unsingular
      unknown

In Realms of Day

pressing in from the horizon-ache
smokestacks forceps at the temple
pressing with tonnage hauled on the expressways
Caution when the brake-lights go red

limping-dragged, a foot gone wrong
pressing a pressure like a beat, a beat
off-rhythm
dragged a few inches off-
rhythm like a foot
curiously numb in the nerves

                    Veering this way
casual and unstoppable
jetplane crashlanding lightly on the roof
light as moonlight
veering in a pressure of the old forceps
the pressing-in horizon
of smokestacks flame-rimmed, and water towers, and towers
with turrets indecipherable
in the aluminum-orange glow

downriver from Detroit
it is all the color of a jukebox
gutteral and neon-lit in its belly
tarry stains inhaled press lightly
against the tissue
the sacred sac breathing *Caution*
or maybe not *Caution* at all
but melodies that interrupt the car radio's static
the halfhour drive home
the expressway slowed-down and very flat
the horizon therefore invisible
or someone else's idea
that ends up in a poem

but no poems here

Dreaming America

When the two-lane highway was widened
the animals retreated.
Skunks, raccoons, rabbits—even their small corpses
disappeared from the road—transformed into rags
then into designs
then into stains
then nothing.

When the highway was linked to another
then to another
six lanes then nine then twelve rose
sweeping to the horizon
along measured white lines.
The polled Herefords were sold.
When the cornfields were bulldozed
the farmhouses at their edges turned into shanties;
the outbuildings fell.

When the fields were paved over
Frisch's Big Boy rose seventy-five feet in the air.
The *Sunoco* and *Texaco* and *Gulf* signs competed
on hundred-foot stilts
like eyeballs on stalks
white optic-nerves
miraculous.
Illuminated at night.

Where the useless stretch of trees lay
an orange sphere like a golf ball
announces the Shopping Mall, open
for Thursday evening shopping.
There, tonight, droves of teenagers hunt
one another, alert on the memorized pavement.

Where did the country go?—cry the travelers, soaring
past. *Where did the country go?*—ask the strangers.
The teenagers never ask.

Where horses grazed in a dream that had no history,
tonight a thirteen-year-old girl stands dreaming
into the window of Levitz's Record Shop.
We drive past, in a hurry. We disappear.
We return.

"All Things
Are Full of Gods"

—so Thales spoke
and so we repeat
staggering
in the unity of these broken-
off parts

curious unity of jigsaw
puzzle parts
strewn wide by a playful wind

I, I—godly in disharmony
I plan to resume—
I intend to continue—
I remember with nostalgia—

The pattern shrieks, breaks
recomposes itself
the coil of harmony eludes us
defies and streams through us
I am patient
I am waiting
I will triumph.

Waiting

Too many gulls to be counted.
Unrhythmic waves—immense, shallow—
        the sucking noises never predictable.
He waits on the beach, his arms tight around his knees.
He is not a child, he sits too heavily.

A Canada goose flies in, the wings ungainly, noisy.
Seven mallards ride the waves
and there are innumerable sailboats, all silent.
Is this perfection?
He waits for the next wave to change everything.

CPSIA information can be obtained
at www.ICGtesting.com
Printed in the USA
LVHW04s1053130518
577027LV00001B/181/P